MAN
IS NOT MADE FOR DEFEAT
A MAN CAN BE DESTROYED BUT NOT DEFEATED

LUCK IS A
THING THAT COMES
IN MANY FORMS AND WHO
CAN RECOGNIZE HER?

dreams do come true if only we wish hard enough

THE MOMENT YOU DOUBT WHETHER YOU CAN FLY YOU CEASE FOR EVER TO BE ABLE TO DO IT

NEVER SAY GOODBYE BECAUSE GOODBYE MEANS GOING AWAY AND GOING AWAY MEANS FORGETTING.

IT DOESN'T MATTER IF YOU'RE BORN IN A DUCK YARD,
SO LONG AS YOU ARE HATCHED FROM A SWAN'S EGG.

DEEP DOWN, EVERYBODY'S
BEAUTIFUL? - NO,
EVERYBODY'S UGLY.

talk not to me of blasphemy, man; I'd strike the sun if it insulted me

NEVER STAND BEGGING
FOR THAT WHICH YOU
HAVE THE POWER TO EARN

THERE IS
NOTHING NEW
UNDER THE SUN
IT HAS ALL BEEN
DONE BEFORE

AS SOON AS YOU TRUST YOURSELF,
YOU WILL KNOW HOW TO LIVE.

MAN IS NOT MADE FOR DEFEAT.
A MAN CAN BE DESTROYED BUT NOT DEFEATED.

IF THE OTHERS HEARD ME TALKING OUT LOUD
THEY WOULD THINK THAT I AM CRAZY.
BUT SINCE I AM NOT, I DO NOT CARE.

LUCK IS A
THING THAT COMES
IN MANY FORMS AND WHO
CAN RECOGNIZE HER?

RESPECT WAS INVENTED TO COVER THE EMPTY PLACE WHERE LOVE SHOULD BE

ALL HAPPY FAMILIES ARE ALIKE. EACH UNHAPPY FAMILY IS UNHAPPY IN IT'S OWN WAY

IF YOU LOOK FOR PERFECTION YOU'LL NEVER BE CONTENT

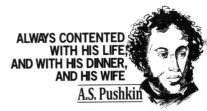

ALWAYS CONTENTED
WITH HIS LIFE,
AND WITH HIS DINNER,
AND HIS WIFE
A.S. Pushkin

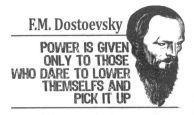

F.M. Dostoevsky

POWER IS GIVEN
ONLY TO THOSE
WHO DARE TO LOWER
THEMSELFS AND
PICK IT UP

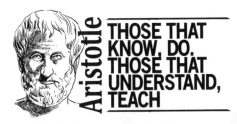

Aristotle

THOSE THAT KNOW, DO. THOSE THAT UNDERSTAND, TEACH

dreams
do come
true
if only we wish
hard enough

THE MOMENT YOU DOUBT WHETHER YOU CAN FLY YOU CEASE FOR EVER TO BE ABLE TO DO IT

NEVER SAY GOODBYE
BECAUSE GOODBYE MEANS GOING AWAY AND GOING AWAY
MEANS FORGETTING.

IT DOESN'T MATTER IF YOU'RE BORN IN A DUCK YARD, SO LONG AS YOU ARE HATCHED FROM A SWAN'S EGG.

DEEP DOWN, EVERYBODY'S BEAUTIFUL? NO. EVERYBODY'S UGLY.

Talk not to me of blasphemy, man; I'd strike the sun if it insulted me

NEVER STAND BEGGING
FOR THAT WHICH YOU
HAVE THE POWER TO EARN

AS SOON AS YOU TRUST YOURSELF,
YOU WILL KNOW HOW TO LIVE.

MAN IS NOT MADE FOR DEFEAT. A MAN CAN BE DESTROYED BUT NOT DEFEATED.

IF THE OTHERS HEARD ME TALKING OUT LOUD
THEY WOULD THINK THAT I AM CRAZY.
BUT SINCE I AM NOT, I DO NOT CARE

LUCK IS A
THING THAT COMES
IN MANY FORMS AND WHO
CAN RECOGNIZE HER?

RESPECT WAS INVENTED TO COVER THE EMPTY PLACE WHERE LOVE SHOULD BE

WHERE LOVE SHOULD BE

ALL HAPPY FAMILIES ARE ALIKE; EACH UNHAPPY FAMILY IS UNHAPPY IN IT'S OWN WAY

IF YOU LOOK FOR PERFECTION
YOU'LL NEVER BE CONTENT

ALWAYS CONTENTED
WITH HIS LIFE,
AND WITH HIS DINNER,
AND HIS WIFE

A.S. Pushkin

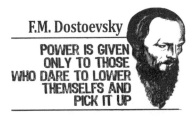
F.M. Dostoevsky

POWER IS GIVEN
ONLY TO THOSE
WHO DARE TO LOWER
THEMSELFS AND
PICK IT UP

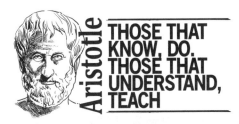

Aristotle

THOSE THAT
KNOW, DO.
THOSE THAT
UNDERSTAND,
TEACH

IT DOESN'T MATTER IF YOU'RE BORN IN A DUCK YARD, SO LONG AS YOU ARE HATCHED FROM A SWAN'S EGG.

"DEEP DOWN, EVERYBODY'S... BEAUTIFUL? - NO. EVERYBODY'S UGLY.

Talk not to me of blasphemy, man; I'd strike the sun if it insulted me

NEVER STAND BEGGING
FOR THAT WHICH YOU
HAVE THE POWER TO EARN

THERE IS
NOTHING NEW
UNDER THE SUN
IT HAS ALL BEEN
DONE BEFORE

AS SOON AS YOU TRUST YOURSELF,
YOU WILL KNOW HOW TO LIVE.

IF THE OTHERS HEARD ME TALKING OUT LOUD
THEY WOULD THINK THAT I AM CRAZY.
BUT SINCE I AM NOT, I DO NOT CARE

MAN
IS NOT MADE FOR DEFEAT.
A MAN CAN BE DESTROYED BUT NOT DEFEATED

LUCK IS A
THING THAT COMES
IN MANY FORMS AND WHO
CAN RECOGNIZE HER?

RESPECT WAS INVENTED TO COVER THE EMPTY PLACE WHERE LOVE SHOULD BE

WHERE LOVE SHOULD BE

ALL HAPPY FAMILIES ARE ALIKE; EACH UNHAPPY FAMILY IS UNHAPPY IN IT'S OWN WAY

IF YOU LOOK FOR PERFECTION YOU'LL NEVER BE CONTENT

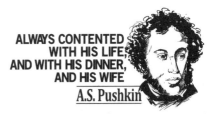

ALWAYS CONTENTED
WITH HIS LIFE,
AND WITH HIS DINNER,
AND HIS WIFE

A.S. Pushkin

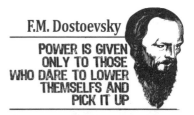

F.M. Dostoevsky

POWER IS GIVEN
ONLY TO THOSE
WHO DARE TO LOWER
THEMSELFS AND
PICK IT UP

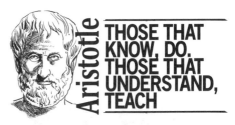
Aristotle

THOSE THAT
KNOW, DO.
THOSE THAT
UNDERSTAND,
TEACH

dreams do come **true** if only we wish hard enough

THE MOMENT YOU DOUBT WHETHER YOU CAN FLY YOU CEASE FOR EVER TO BE ABLE TO DO IT

NEVER SAY GOODBYE BECAUSE GOODBYE MEANS GOING AWAY AND GOING AWAY MEANS FORGETTING.

IT DOESN'T MATTER IF YOU'RE BORN IN A DUCK YARD, SO LONG AS YOU ARE HATCHED FROM A SWAN'S EGG

DEEP DOWN, EVERYBODY'S... BEAUTIFUL? - NO. EVERYBODY'S UGLY.

NEVER STAND BEGGING
FOR THAT WHICH YOU
HAVE THE POWER TO EARN

THERE IS
NOTHING NEW
UNDER THE SUN.
IT HAS ALL BEEN
DONE BEFORE.

AS SOON AS YOU TRUST YOURSELF,
YOU WILL KNOW HOW TO LIVE.

IF THE OTHERS HEARD ME TALKING OUT LOUD
THEY WOULD THINK THAT I AM CRAZY
BUT SINCE I AM NOT, I DO NOT CARE.

MAN
IS NOT MADE FOR DEFEAT.
A MAN CAN BE DESTROYED BUT NOT DEFEATED

LUCK IS A
THING THAT COMES
IN MANY FORMS AND WHO
CAN RECOGNIZE HER?

RESPECT WAS INVENTED TO COVER THE EMPTY PLACE WHERE LOVE SHOULD BE

IF YOU LOOK FOR PERFECTION YOU'LL NEVER BE CONTENT

ALL HAPPY FAMILIES ARE ALIKE; EACH UNHAPPY FAMILY IS UNHAPPY IN IT'S OWN WAY

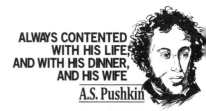

ALWAYS CONTENTED
WITH HIS LIFE,
AND WITH HIS DINNER,
AND HIS WIFE

A.S. Pushkin

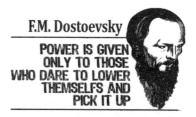

F.M. Dostoevsky

POWER IS GIVEN
ONLY TO THOSE
WHO DARE TO LOWER
THEMSELFS AND
PICK IT UP

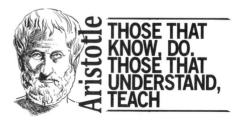

Aristotle

THOSE THAT KNOW, DO. THOSE THAT UNDERSTAND, TEACH

dreams
do come
true
if only we wish
hard enough

THE MOMENT
YOU DOUBT WHETHER
YOU CAN FLY YOU CEASE
FOR EVER TO BE
ABLE TO DO IT

NEVER SAY GOODBYE
BECAUSE GOODBYE MEANS GOING AWAY AND GOING AWAY
MEANS FORGETTING.

IT DOESN'T MATTER IF YOU'RE BORN IN A DUCK YARD, SO LONG AS YOU ARE HATCHED FROM A SWAN'S EGG.

DEEP DOWN, EVERYBODY'S... BEAUTIFUL? - NO, EVERYBODY'S UGLY.

NEVER STAND BEGGING
FOR THAT WHICH YOU
HAVE THE POWER TO EARN

THERE IS
NOTHING NEW
UNDER THE SUN.
IT HAS ALL BEEN
DONE BEFORE.

AS SOON AS YOU TRUST YOURSELF,
YOU WILL KNOW HOW TO LIVE.

MAN IS NOT MADE FOR DEFEAT. A MAN CAN BE DESTROYED BUT NOT DEFEATED

IF THE OTHERS HEARD ME TALKING OUT LOUD THEY WOULD THINK THAT I AM CRAZY. BUT SINCE I AM NOT, I DO NOT CARE

LUCK IS A THING THAT COMES IN MANY FORMS AND WHO CAN RECOGNIZE HER?

RESPECT WAS INVENTED TO COVER THE EMPTY PLACE WHERE LOVE SHOULD BE

ALL HAPPY FAMILIES ARE ALIKE; EACH UNHAPPY FAMILY IS UNHAPPY IN IT'S OWN WAY

IF YOU LOOK FOR PERFECTION YOU'LL NEVER BE CONTENT

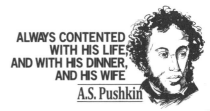

ALWAYS CONTENTED
WITH HIS LIFE,
AND WITH HIS DINNER,
AND HIS WIFE

A.S. Pushkin

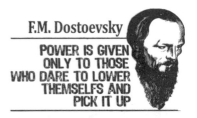

F.M. Dostoevsky

POWER IS GIVEN
ONLY TO THOSE
WHO DARE TO LOWER
THEMSELFS AND
PICK IT UP

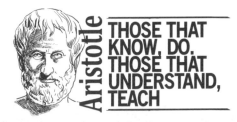

THOSE THAT KNOW, DO. THOSE THAT UNDERSTAND, TEACH

Aristotle

dreams
do come
true
if only we wish
hard enough

THE MOMENT
YOU DOUBT WHETHER
YOU CAN FLY YOU CEASE
FOR EVER TO BE
ABLE TO DO IT

NEVER SAY GOODBYE
BECAUSE GOODBYE MEANS GOING AWAY AND GOING AWAY
MEANS FORGETTING.

IT DOESN'T MATTER IF YOU'RE BORN IN A DUCK YARD, SO LONG AS YOU ARE HATCHED FROM A SWAN'S EGG.

"DEEP DOWN, EVERYBODY'S... BEAUTIFUL." - NO. EVERYBODY'S UGLY.

NEVER STAND BEGGING
FOR THAT WHICH YOU
HAVE THE POWER TO EARN

THERE IS
NOTHING NEW
UNDER THE SUN.
IT HAS ALL BEEN
DONE BEFORE

AS SOON AS YOU TRUST YOURSELF,
YOU WILL KNOW HOW TO LIVE.

MAN IS NOT MADE FOR DEFEAT. A MAN CAN BE DESTROYED BUT NOT DEFEATED

IF THE OTHERS HEARD ME TALKING OUT LOUD
THEY WOULD THINK THAT I AM CRAZY.
BUT SINCE I AM NOT, I DO NOT CARE

LUCK IS A
THING THAT COMES
IN MANY FORMS AND WHO
CAN RECOGNIZE HER?

RESPECT WAS INVENTED TO COVER THE EMPTY PLACE WHERE LOVE SHOULD BE

ALL HAPPY FAMILIES ARE ALIKE; EACH UNHAPPY FAMILY IS UNHAPPY IN IT'S OWN WAY

IF YOU LOOK FOR PERFECTION YOU'LL NEVER BE CONTENT

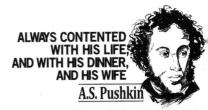

ALWAYS CONTENTED
WITH HIS LIFE,
AND WITH HIS DINNER,
AND HIS WIFE

A.S. Pushkin

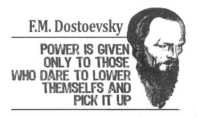

F.M. Dostoevsky

POWER IS GIVEN
ONLY TO THOSE
WHO DARE TO LOWER
THEMSELFS AND
PICK IT UP

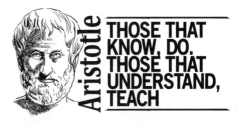

Aristotle

**THOSE THAT
KNOW, DO.
THOSE THAT
UNDERSTAND,
TEACH**